The
Do-It-Yourself
Project Book

Anna Burgess

Illustrated by
Darren Green

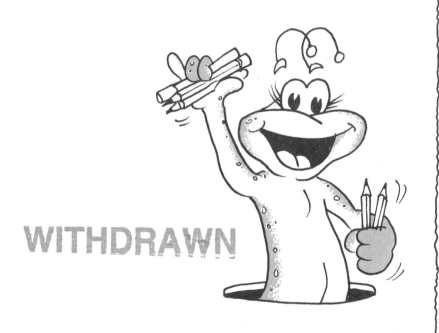

Watermill Press

The Do-It-Yourself Project Book
First published in the United States by Watermill Press,
an imprint of Troll Associates, Inc., 1994.

Text copyright © 1994 by Anna Burgess.
Illustrations copyright © 1994 by Anna Burgess
and Lineup Pty Limited.

Assembly and design by Just James Studio.
Art by Darren Green.

ISBN 0-8167-3343-0

Printed in the United States of America.

10 9 8 7 6 5 4 3

Cataloguing-in-Publication data:

Burgess, Anna.
    The do-it-yourself project book.

    1. Creative activities and seat work - Juvenile literature
    2. Title

649.5

TERRIFIC PROJECTS YOU CAN DO

ou'll probably do hundreds of projects while you're in school. This book shows you how to be more creative with them, so that they will work better for you.

Projects are a great way to get you thinking about what is important in the topics you study in class.

You don't have to be an artist, an engineer or a genius to make a project interesting – but you do have to become a good planner!

Once you've settled on the topic for your project, "walk" through the pages of the DO-IT-YOURSELF PROJECT BOOK and you'll come up with an idea that's just right.

The point is to make others want to look at what you've done and learn from it. This is a great starting point.

STOP! Some of the projects in this book require the use of sharp knives. Please check with an adult before using these.

CONTENTS

START AT THE BEGINNING

Usually your teacher will give you a topic for your project. Sometimes you'll be the one to decide. Once you've got the topic worked out, you can start thinking about how you'll present the information.

Let's say that the topic is: "THE LIFE CYCLE OF THE BUTTERFLY".
- Define (or state) your objective – what it is you want to communicate. It might be: "To show all of the stages of the butterfly from egg to wings".
- Now choose the format – the way of presenting information – that suits.

Let's say you choose to make a TV "film" and record the story on a cassette recorder. (Remember, this is just one way of presenting your project – you may choose to do a poster, a wall chart, a diorama or any of the other examples in this book.) First though, comes the research – getting the facts about your topic and finding pictures you can use for your illustrations.

RESEARCH.

Where to go for information?

These are just some of the places where you might find articles or pictures on your topic.

You might think of others...

When you find information that is interesting and related to your project theme, you can:

- make notes (you don't have to write sentences at this stage, key words will do)
- photocopy (if it's a book)
- cut out (if it's a magazine)
- trace (if it's an illustration or photograph)

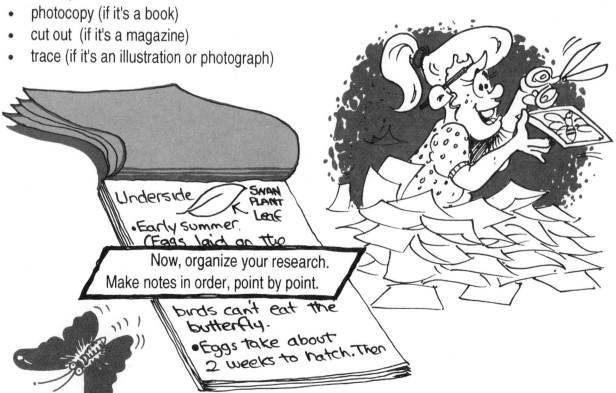

Now, organize your research.
Make notes in order, point by point.

WHERE TO START?

Filmmakers start with a "story board" – and so can you! On a large sheet rough out the pictures that will go in each "frame" of your TV film.

You are going to do a picture for each frame on your "strip" of "film".
What kind of artwork will be best? These are just some of the choices you've got.

colored Pencils

felt tipped pens

paint

crayon

collage

potato print

photography

roller print

Crayon and dye...

You might think of others...

Complete the pictures, using your research to get them right. (Make sure the sheets you use are all the same size and shape.)

GETTING IT TOGETHER

Join the pictures into a "strip". (All pictures facing the same way.)
(To make the TV screen, turn to pages 44 – 45 of this book)

You'll need a script for the story you're going to record on the cassette recorder. A script is the words you will say to describe each of the pictures that will come up on the "screen". For each picture, write 3 – 4 sentences. Tell the most important things (or the most interesting things) about each. Do a draft first. Say the words out loud as you write them. When it sounds just right, print the sentences on cards - one for each picture. Now record. (Get an adult to help here, if you need to.)

TURN ROD & WIND PICTURES THROUGH TO VIEW.

TO USE
• PRESS PLAY
• WIND TOP ONLY TO TURN FILM
• PLEASE REWIND TAPE AND FILM STRIP

THANKS BILL

Your finished project.

POSTERS - KEEPING IT SIMPLE

Posters are great for getting your message across. (They say a picture's worth a thousand words!) Your project might be a poster or a series of posters. The best posters are strong and simple, with a message that people will remember.

Here are some ideas to get you thinking:

$AVE POWER

No Fires

DRIPS WASTE WATER

THIS FUR COAT BELONGS TO A DUMB ANIMAL

WALL CHARTS [First Cousins of Posters]

Sometimes it's easier to say things with pictures than with words. A wall chart is a labeled picture or diagram that gives you information. First sort out the information you want to give. Work out how it should be presented. Sketch the artwork as large as possible. Think up labels that will tell the story - a word or two for each can do. Choose the best medium (crayons, paint, collage, etc.) and complete the wall chart.

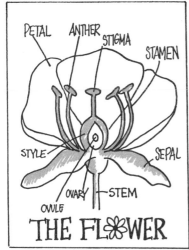

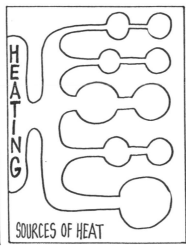

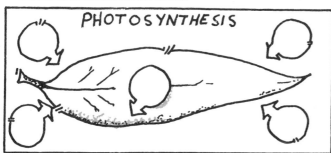

Headings can attract attention to your wall chart. Use creative lettering that suits the topic. (See the Do-It-Yourself Lettering Book for examples)

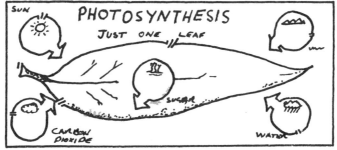

Smaller headings - called subheadings - can help people to understand what you're getting at. Add pictures for interest.

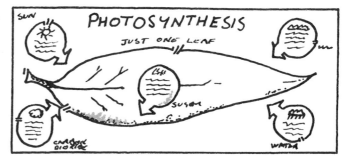

Write small blocks of information made up of important facts to make your wall chart informative.

BE DESIGNING...

Wall charts that are well designed and easy to follow are what you should aim for.

Layout is important. (Layout is where things go on the sheet of paper).

Arrows and lines show how one part of the chart connects to the other. You can use different kinds of arrows and lines to show different things.

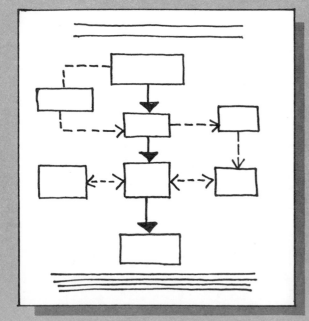

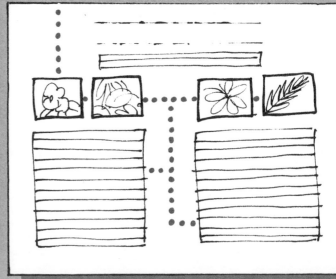

KEEPING YOUR BALANCE

Good wall charts have balance. Balance means having the right "mix" of all of the parts: *text *headings *outline shapes *lines *illustrations.

Good layout makes it easier to get your information across. We read from the top of a page to the bottom and from the left-hand side of a page to the right. So put something strong at the top of your chart - a heading, a box, or a picture - so that you catch people's eyes. Your chart can be laid out any way you like, as long as it looks pleasing.

Here are some different layouts to get you thinking...

FRAME UP

Borders or frames help to focus your eyes on a poster or page.
When you design your layout, think about where a border might go.

Decorative borders add special interest.
Think of some design element connected
with your topic, and use it to make an interesting border.

Borders can be used to highlight
just some part of your text.

(See the 'D.I.Y. Lettering Book' for lots of great ideas for borders).

GRABBING ATTENTION

We want people to look at our projects, so we have to grab their attention.
One way to do this is with a decorative title.

This "shape book" title
is based on the
shape of the Earth.

Choose the title for your book, page or poster.
What shape letters does it make you think of?

How wiil you put the words together?

Do rough sketches with a pencil until you get the "feel" of it.

This heading shows the ugliness of pollution.

And this one adds some fun to your heading.

(See the 'Do It Yourself Lettering Book' for more creative lettering ideas).

MAKE YOUR OWN BOOK

For projects, you can use blank paged books you buy at the store or you can add that special touch by making your own.

CASED BOOKS

You'll need:

- stiff cardboard
- strong paper (for outside cover)
- strong paper (for inside cover lining)
- strong liquid or stick glue
- bookbinding material
- paper for pages
- stapler

1. Decide how big your pages will be.
   Cut paper twice that size.
   Fold and "batch" in, say "10s".
   Staple each batch near the fold.

2. Cut 2 pieces of cardboard 1/4 inch (1 cm) larger than the page size. Cut 3 strips of cardboard the length of the cover, 1 as wide as you need for the spine, and 2 about 1 – 1 1/2 inches (2.5 - 4 cm) wide.

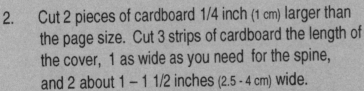

3. Cut cover paper 3/4 – 1 1/2 inches (2 - 4 cm) larger than the cover boards. Glue flaps onto boards and let dry.

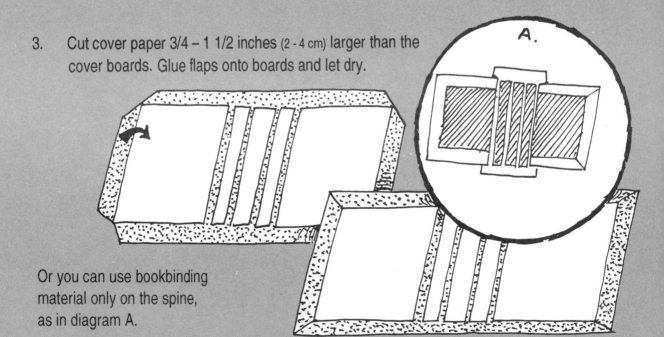

A.

Or you can use bookbinding material only on the spine, as in diagram A.

4. Use patterned paper or decorate your own for lining.
Cut the cover lining 3/4 inch (1.5 cm) smaller than cover and glue in place.

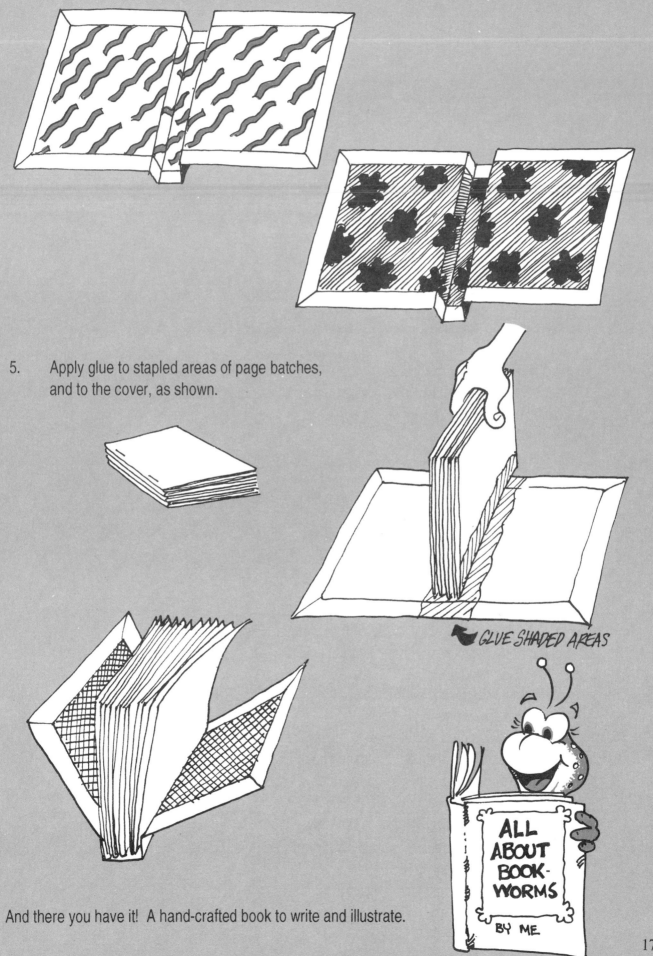

5. Apply glue to stapled areas of page batches, and to the cover, as shown.

GLUE SHADED AREAS

And there you have it! A hand-crafted book to write and illustrate.

ALL ABOUT BOOK-WORMS

BY ME

SOME OTHER WAYS

- **Tie-bind**
1   Make a cover as shown on pages 16 – 17.
2   Punch 2 holes along the back spine flap.
3   Punch holes in your batch of pages.
4   Thread ribbon or string through holes and tie pages in place.

- **Loose-leaf**
1   Make two separate covers, with spine flaps, but no spine.
2   Punch holes in the flaps.
3   Punch holes in your batch of pages.
4   Tie with string, pipe cleaners or ribbon.

- **Staple books**
1   Cover board with decorated paper
2   Fold and put pages in place
3   Staple along the outside fold

- **Split pin books**
1   Cover 2 pieces of board to make covers
2   Punch holes on edges of covers and pages
3   Fasten with "split pins".

- **Shape books**

Books are normally oblong or square in shape, but you
can create books in any shape you like, to suit your topic.

Look back to the "All About the Planet Earth" book on page 15.
It's round like the planet.

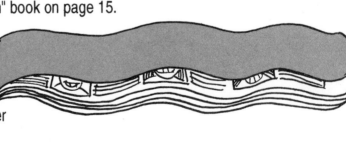

- To make a shape book:

1   Choose strong cardboard for the cover
2   Fold it to make a spine.
3   Draw your shape and cut through both layers of the cover.
    (You can cut the front, then trace onto the back and cut.)
4   Position the folded pages on the open cover.
5   Stitch the pages in like this, one sheet at a time.
6   Use a darning needle and wool or thick thread.
    (Stitch loosely until you have finished, then gently tighten and
    make a knot to fasten.)

This shape book would be great for a project on worms,
snakes or waves - or, what else?

SHAPING UP

Here are just a few ideas to get you thinking:

These sorts of shapes can be used for lots of different topics.

Fold back your covers near the spine, so that pages can easily be opened.

Concertina books

You'll need:

* sheets of paper or light board, folded in half
* strips of paper for joins
* strong glue

You can make these books as long as you like.

Cut strips of paper the length of the page and about 3/4 - 1 inch (2 - 3 cm) wide. Join the pages as shown, always joining the cut edges.

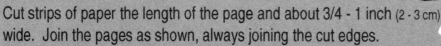
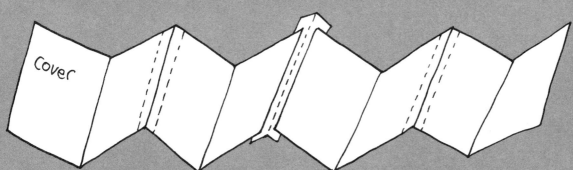

THE BIG COVER UP

You *can* tell a book by its cover! Make the cover interesting and people will want to look inside.

Book covers usually have:

- Title (or name) of the topic or story.
- Author's name (in this case, yours!)

They may have:

- A subtitle (or heading that explains a bit more about the contents)
- A picture or drawing to do with the contents
- A decorative border
- A title on the spine of a bound book
- A "logo" - the little sign or symbol that you invent to put on your very own books

A catchy title can make all the difference in the world to an everyday subject.

CREATIVE COVERS

Use these and other ideas to make your covers the BEST.
Use strong glue to add interesting bits and pieces to your covers.

STICK ON REAL FLOWERS & LEAVES

SPELL THE WORD OUT IN GLUE & SPRINKLE SAND OVER THE GLUE.

Stick on real leaves, grasses and flowers and cover with plastic.

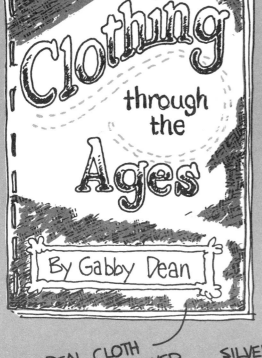

CUT LETTERS OUT OF MAGAZINES TO MAKE WORDS.

Cut lettering and pictures out of colored paper.

REAL CLOTH GLUED TO COVER

SILVER FOIL STARS

A knife is useful, but take great care with it.
Corrugated cardboard, plastic sponge, leather, carpet off-cuts, pieces of wool or even crushed eggshells can be glued on to your cover to create interesting textures and patterns.

BETWEEN THE COVERS

The "Contents" page is a list of topics in a book. It is placed near the front. Page numbers are shown for each section or chapter.

Contents pages can be decorative or straightforward. You decide.
Here are two examples to get you thinking.

An "Index" is an alphabetical list of important things mentioned in the book. It is usually at the back of the book. It is a quick way to find something you're looking for.

INDEX

Tabs can be used to find sections in a longer book. You can buy tabs or make them yourself.

SPIDER FACTS
C.WEBB

TYPES
HABITAT
FOODS

TYPES
HABITAT
FOOD
CYCLES
ENEMIES
GENERAL
SPECIES

The black widow spider has a distinctive mark on its belly.

21

BOOK WORMS DON'T HAVE FEET...

The bottom of a page is called the "foot". A "footnote" is an explanation you put at the bottom of the page, instead of making your text too long and complicated.

23

GETTING GRAPHIC

Graphs or Charts are wonderful ways of saving words. Shapes, pictures and labels can tell readers a lot very simply.

There are many kinds of graph. All graphs show the relationships between numbers. For example:

If there are 17 people in your class, 7 boys and 10 girls, this is how you could graph the information.

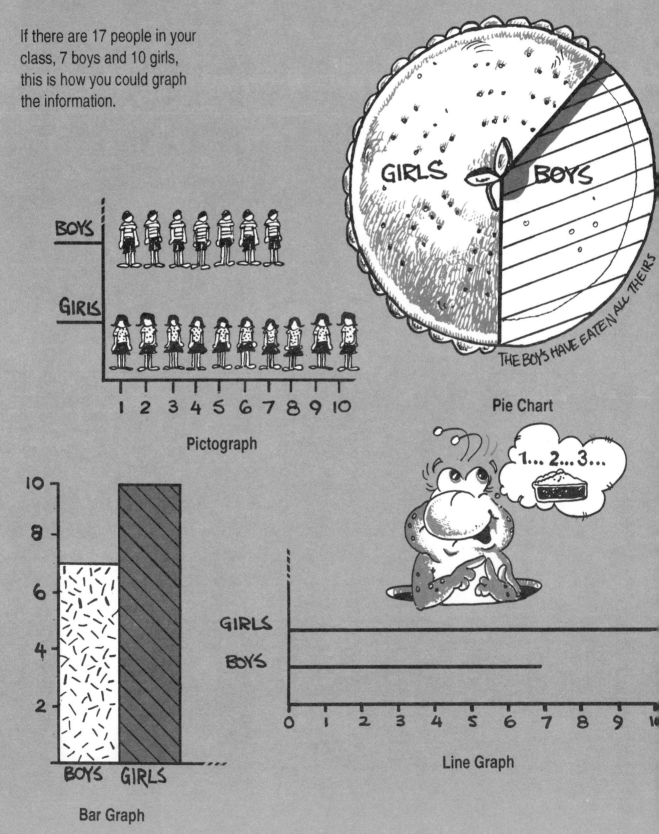

Pie Chart

THE BOYS HAVE EATEN ALL THEIRS

BOYS

GIRLS

1 2 3 4 5 6 7 8 9 10

Pictograph

1... 2... 3...

GIRLS

BOYS

0 1 2 3 4 5 6 7 8 9 10

Line Graph

BOYS GIRLS

Bar Graph

A GRAPH CAN BE A PIECE OF CAKE!

Say your project is about eating habits in your school. You do a survey, asking questions about favorite fast foods. You've got the answers, but how do you communicate them? What better way than with a pie chart?

The "pieces" of the pie chart each represent a percentage of the whole.

There are other ways of graphing survey results. Here are some ideas:

Survey of eye colors in our class.

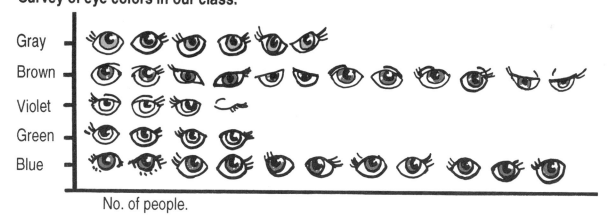

No. of people.

Survey of families with pets.

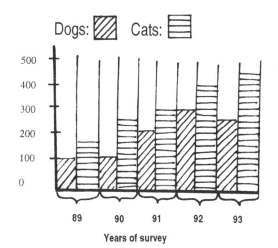

Flowers exported.

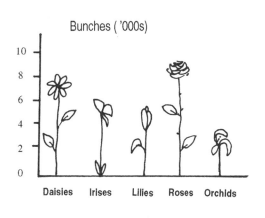

LET DIAGRAMS DO THE WORK

You can have a simple outline sketch with labels.

OR a complex diagram with brief explanations.

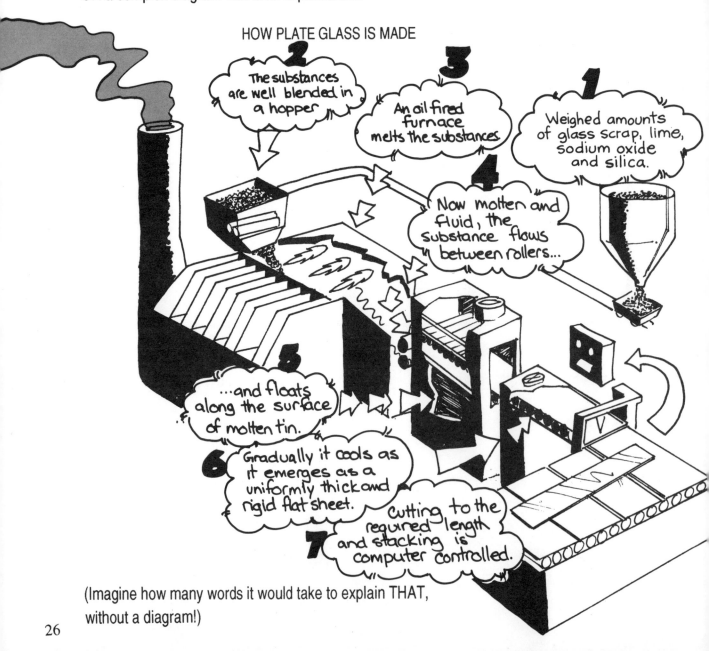

(Imagine how many words it would take to explain THAT,

without a diagram!)

BE A POP-UP ENGINEER

Pop-up books are favorites and are fun to make. They take a fair bit of planning, so allow plenty of time.

You'll need:

- a double page sheet of strong paper
- very light cardboard for model
- cutting knife or scissors
- paints or crayons
- strong glue

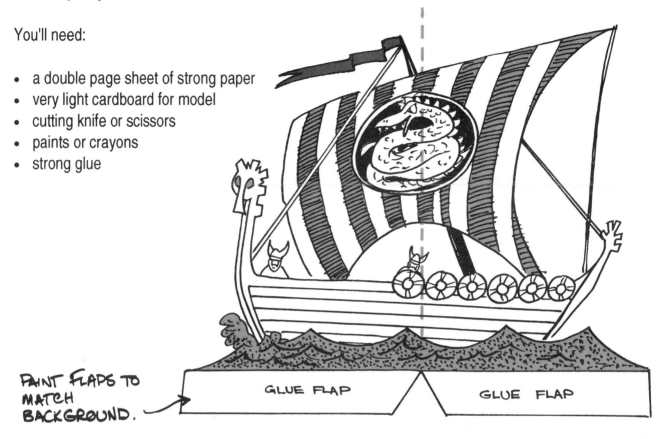

PAINT FLAPS TO MATCH BACKGROUND.

GLUE FLAP

GLUE FLAP

We show you how to make a pop-up Viking ship, but it could be anything you like.

1. Draw the ship, with the flaps each about 1 inch (2.5 cm) less than the width of the page. Make the ship about as tall as half the height of the page.

2. Color the ship and cut it out.
Fold the flaps on the dotted lines.

3. Color the background page.

4. Glue the ship flaps at an angle on the double page spread. Make sure you get the angle right, so that the ship pops up when you open the pages.

5. Paint over the flaps to match the background.

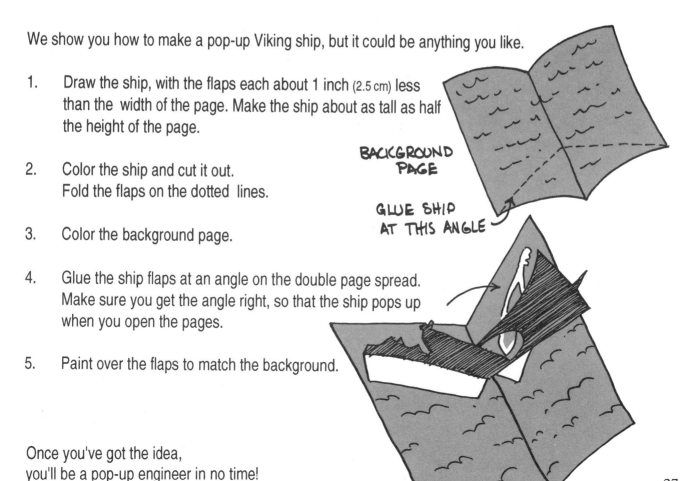

BACKGROUND PAGE

GLUE SHIP AT THIS ANGLE

Once you've got the idea,
you'll be a pop-up engineer in no time!

KEEPING TABS ON BOOKS

Tabs make it possible to move things in books. They all work by means of "arms" that move between two pages.

First, let's try a door that opens.
You'll need:

- 3 sheets of strong paper each about
  8 by 11 1/2 inches (21 - 29 cm)
- scissors and a cutting knife
- glue

1. Fold two of the sheets of paper in half on the long side.

2. On one, make 2 slits, 4 inches (10 cm) apart.
   Label these A and B.   (See diagram.)

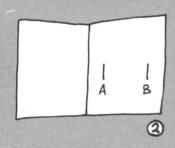

②

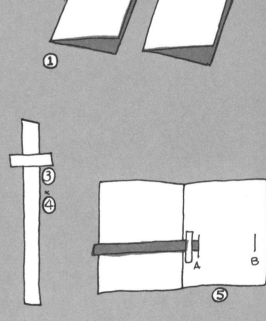

3. From the third sheet cut a strip 7 by 1/2 inch (18 - 1.5 cm)
   and another 1 1/2 by 1/2 inch (4 - 1.5 cm).

4. Glue the small strip across the long strip, 1 inch (2.5 cm)
   from the end (so that you make a tall letter 't'.)

5. Push the short end, from the left, through slit A.
   (It will only go as far as the 't' bar.)

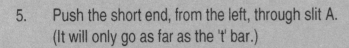

6. Fold the long end back and through slit B.

7. Glue the second sheet of paper over the first.
   (Glue only around the edges.)

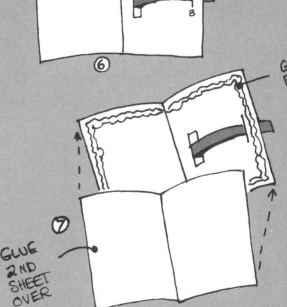

GLUE
2ND
SHEET
OVER

8. Cut a smaller bit of paper for your "door". Fold it in half and glue onto small flap c then glue together.

"Doors" can make birthday cards more fun, too.

KEEPING TABS ON YOUR PROJECTS

A simple slide tab can be used to brighten up your project. Let's say your project is about rabbits. A tab cover like the one on this page will certainly get people's interest.

You'll need:

- 2 sheets of strong paper each about 8 by 11 1/2 inches (21 - 29 cm)
- 1 strip of paper about 8 by 1/2 inch (21 - 2 cm) and one 2 by 3/4 inch (6 - 2 cm)
- scissors and a cutting knife
- glue

1. Make a diagonal slash on 1 piece of paper (see diagram).

2. Draw your picture, and cut the slit down to the rabbit burrow.

3. Make the slide by gluing the short strip of paper at the end of the long strip.
Fold the short strip back over the slide and put the slide in the slit.

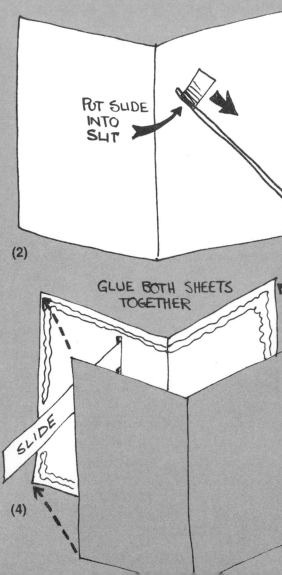

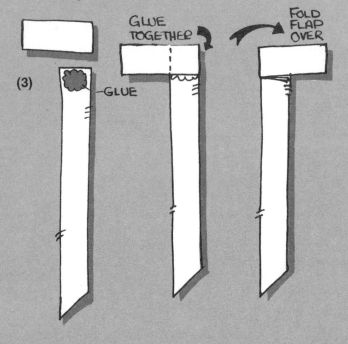

4. Glue the second sheet to the back of the first, making sure that the slide can move.

5. Draw and cut out the mother rabbit and glue to the slide flap.

(5) MOTHER RABBIT

BABY RABBITS

When it comes to feeding her babies, This mother is no bunny!

FLYING OBJECTS - SET UP A JET

Your project may be about flight and you decide to make models of airplanes through history. Here's how you can make a jet fighter. This will give you ideas for making other models.

You'll need:

- cardboard tubes (narrow and wide)
- light cardboard (corrugated cardboard for "wheels")
- scissors and strong glue
- paint for decorating

1. Choose 3 small tubes for "wheel legs" and 4 slightly larger ones for "engines".

2. Draw and cut out all the body parts shown. (If you want a larger model, make sure you make all parts bigger - to scale - see page 64).

3. Glue together, paint and decorate.

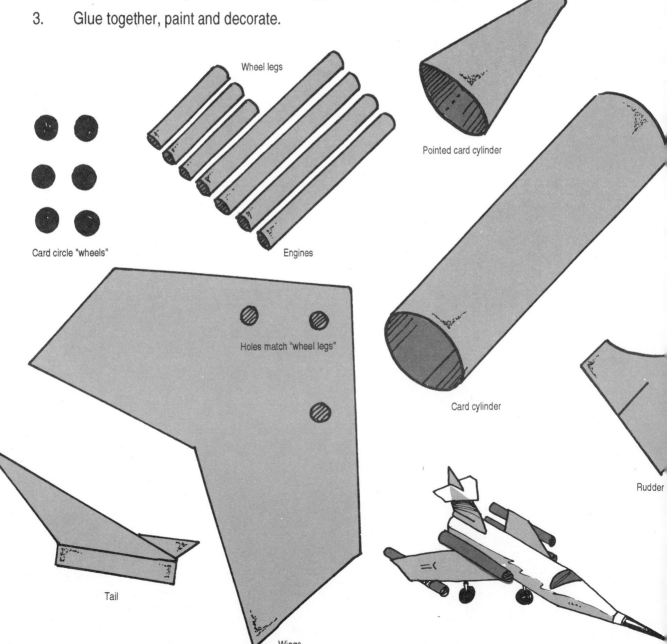

Wheel legs

Pointed card cylinder

Card circle "wheels"

Engines

Holes match "wheel legs"

Card cylinder

Rudder

Tail

Wings

BOAST ABOUT YOUR KITE!

Say your project is about a different kind of flight. You could build kites and demonstrate how they fly. There are dozens of ways to make kites. Here is one. Just remember that kites need to be light and have a flat surface to "catch the wind".

You'll need:

- 2 thin dowels (one twice as long as the other) with grooves cut in ends
- lots of string
- large sheet of paper (newspaper will do)
- a safe cutting knife
- strong glue
- paints, colored paper, etc., to decorate

1. Bind the 2 dowels with string to make a cross.
2. Thread string tightly around the grooves at the ends of the dowels and tie with a knot.

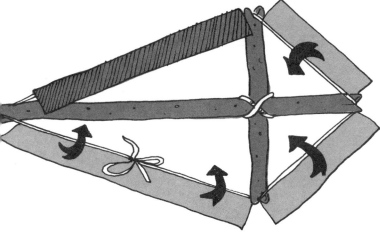

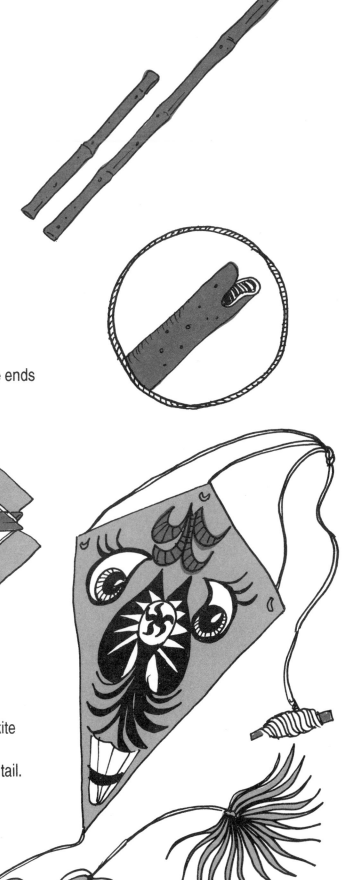

3. Place frame on large sheet of paper. Trim the paper, as shown.
4. Fold edges over firmly and glue.
5. Tie 3 lengths of string to the top corners of the kite frame (as shown). Add long string for flying.
6. Decorate the "face" of your kite and then add a tail.

[Stay away from overhead wires when flying your kite. Who wants to be barbecued?]

TIME LINES

If your project happens to be about things that happened in history or about someone's life, you can create a time line.

A time line can be as simple as a line marked off in years, with important events marked.

1. To create a time line, you need to research, research, research. Read and make notes of the dates of important events related to your subject.

2. Make your notes into very short statements, each on a separate bit of paper. Sort the notes into time order.

3. Mark a line with dates evenly spread on a long strip of paper.

4. Print your notes on the time line, starting with the earliest date.

Apollo Space Flights

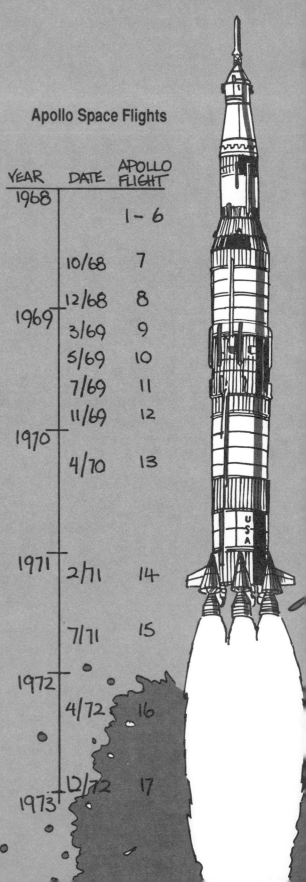

YEAR	DATE	APOLLO FLIGHT
1968		
		1 - 6
	10/68	7
	12/68	8
1969	3/69	9
	5/69	10
	7/69	11
	11/69	12
1970		
	4/70	13
1971	2/71	14
	7/71	15
1972		
	4/72	16
	12/72	17
1973		

ALEXANDER GRAHAM BELL's time line might look like this.
(Read it and you'll find out what he did in 1875 that was really important!)

ALEXANDER GRAHAM BELL BORN IN SCOTLAND 1847	HIS FAMILY WAS DEEPLY INTERESTED IN SPEECH AND DEAFNESS	TRAINED TO TEACH THE DEAF TO SPEAK	STUDIED ANATOMY AND PHYSIOLOGY AND MUSIC	MOVED TO ONTARIO CANADA TO EVADE THREAT OF TUBERCULOSIS 1870
BECAME PROFESSOR OF VOCAL PHYSIOLOGY AT BOSTON UNIVERSITY	BEGAN TO NURTURE THE IDEA OF TRANSMITTING SPEECH ELECTRONICALLY	DISCOVERED THE PRINCIPLE THAT MADE TELEPHONES POSSIBLE 1875	BASIC PATENT FOR DISCOVERY GRANTED 1876	MARRIED MABEL HUBBARD WHO WAS DEAF LIKE HIS MOTHER 1877
HAD MUCH INVOLVEMENT IN FOUNDING THE IMPORTANT MAGAZINE "SCIENCE" 1880	PRESIDENT OF THE NATIONAL GEOGRAPHIC SOCIETY 1898-1904	MADE A REGENT OF THE SMITHSONIAN INSTITUTE 1898	INTERESTS TURNED TO AVIATION AND WAS PATRON OF THE GROUP THAT DEVELOPED THE HYDROFOIL 1907	DIED AN AMERICAN CITIZEN IN NOVIA SCOTIA 1922

PREHISTORIC TIME LINE

		TODAY
CENOZOIC (RECENT LIFE) MAMMALS AND BIRDS APPEAR. 	Quaternary	
	Tertiary	2
MESOZOIC (MIDDLE LIFE) DINOSAURS BECOME EXTINCT.	Cretaceous	65
	Jurassic	135
 FIRST DINOSAURS APPEAR	Triassic	190
PALEOZOIC (OLD LIFE) FIRST LIFE FORMS APPEAR. 		225
		600

Dates shown in millions of years ago.

WHAT'S IN YOUR DAY?

Make a personal time line.

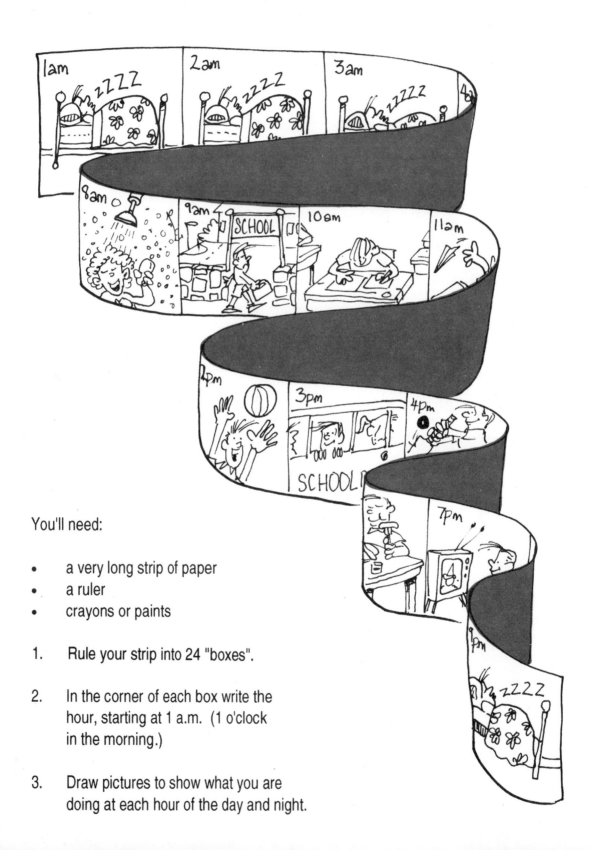

You'll need:

- a very long strip of paper
- a ruler
- crayons or paints

1. Rule your strip into 24 "boxes".

2. In the corner of each box write the
    hour, starting at 1 a.m. (1 o'clock
    in the morning.)

3. Draw pictures to show what you are
    doing at each hour of the day and night.

LIFE LINE

Ask your family to help you do a time line of your life so far.
For example John's looks like this:

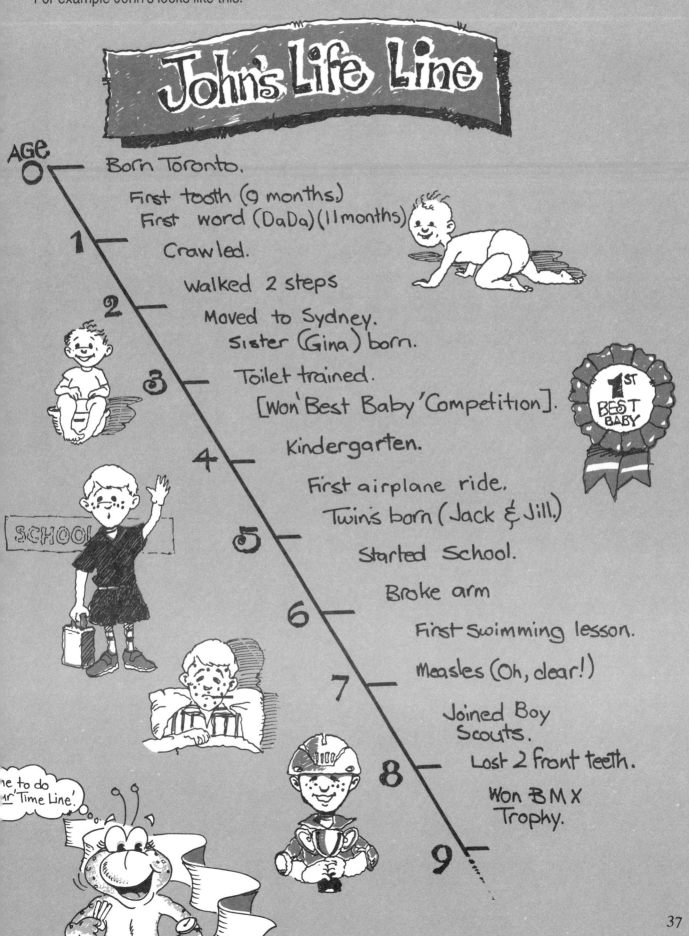

John's Life Line

AGE

0 — Born Toronto.

First tooth (9 months.)
First word (DaDa) (11 months)

1 — Crawled.

Walked 2 steps

2 — Moved to Sydney.
Sister (Gina) born.

3 — Toilet trained.
[Won 'Best Baby' Competition].

Kindergarten.

4 — First airplane ride.
Twins born (Jack & Jill.)

5 — Started School.

Broke arm

6 — First swimming lesson.

Measles (Oh, dear!)

7 — Joined Boy Scouts.
Lost 2 front teeth.

8 — Won BMX Trophy.

9

1ST BEST BABY

SCHOOL

...e to do
...r 'Time Line'.

DIORAMAS (or LIFE IN A SHOE BOX)

Say your project topic is "dinosaurs", and you decide to show how they lived using a 3-D (three dimensional) approach.

Plan ahead:

First do your research. Then sketch how you want your finished diorama to look. What materials will you need? For background? For foreground (the front)? For the cutouts? For the other objects?

You'll need:

- a strip of cardboard (curved to fit the shoe box for the background)
- a small quantity of sand or sawdust, stones, twigs, leaves, etc.
- a shoe box • scissors • wire • paint • household sponge

1. Paint the background.

2. Make foreground things larger. (Gives it a feeling of distance.)

3. Paint some areas with glue and add sand for "earth" or sawdust dyed green for "grass".

4. Use wire and bits of plastic sponge for trees.

5. Trace or draw dinosaur on cardboard and cut out. Decorate. Add stand.

6. Finish off the scene with stones, twigs, and anything else you can find.

7. Make a label, using creative lettering.

THE BIG SCENE (using larger boxes)

Shoe boxes are fine for simple projects. Larger boxes let you show much more detail. Say you're doing a project on cave-dwellers. As always, research first.

1. Create a background. (Why not use Christmas lights for stars?)

2. Make models from clay, plasticine, play dough.

3. Use bits and pieces from everywhere to decorate your scene. (Glue, scissors and paint can do wonders!)

4. Create a label for your diorama: "Cave dwellers, showing animal skin curtain, skin clothes, smoking food, food hanging and tools".

Another project topic might be "Underwater Life on a Coral Reef".

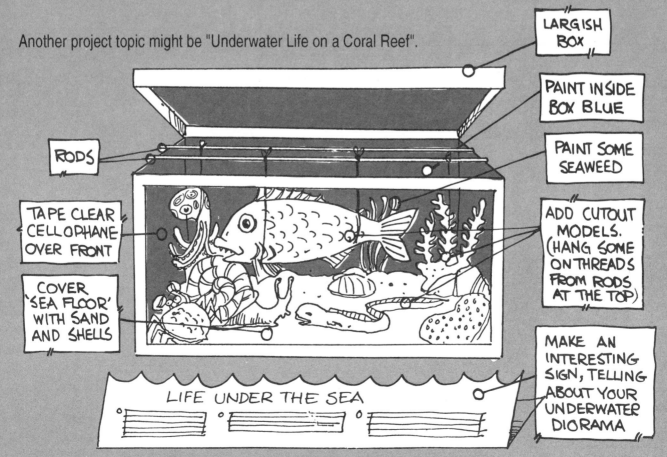

ROLL UP! ROLL UP! ROLL UP!

A scroll is a roll of paper with something written on it. It is just the thing for a story, a poem, a recipe or a list. In olden times, scrolls were used to record special things.

You'll need:

- strong paper that you can roll and unroll many times
- 2 thin round dowels
- cotton reels, table tennis balls, ribbon, wool
- strong glue, thumb tacks or a stapler

1. Tear thick, strong paper, to give a "hand torn" look.
2. Cut dowelling a bit longer than the width of the scroll.
3. Glue a "hem" inwards at both ends of the scroll.
4. When the glue is dry, carefully put dowelling through each end.

Scrolls may be very simple or simply elaborate!

GLUE ON

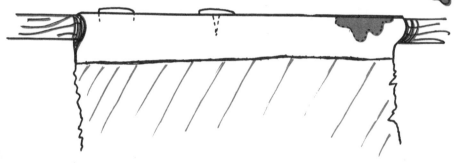

5. Staple, tack or glue the scroll onto the dowelling at both ends.
6. Glue decorations on the ends of the dowelling rods.
7. You could paint them. What about silver or gold?
8. Make tassels by gluing wool onto a small ball, leaving tails (see diagram).

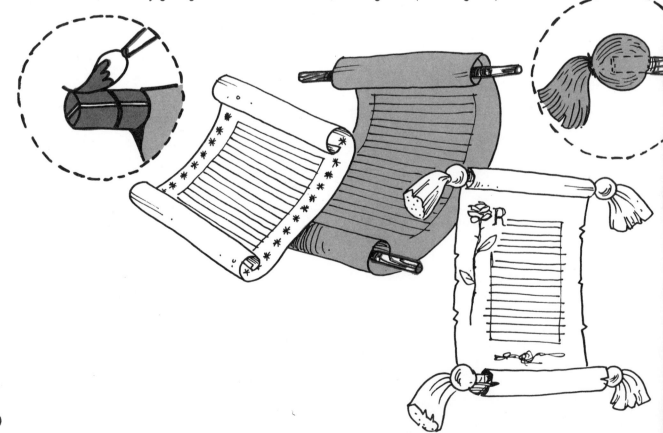

NOTEBOOKS

If your project is one of the 3-D kind, say a diorama, an ant farm or a taped interview, you want to provide information to go along with it. A simple book can do the job.

FOLD & STAPLE

You'll need:

- heavy paper for the cover
- sheets for the "pages"
- a long-armed stapler (or colored wool)

1. Cut cover sheet and pages the same size. Fold, rubbing your thumb along the crease.

2. Put two staples on the outside spine fold, or make two holes, thread the wool and knot it.

3. Write your information in short, easy to read sentences or point form.

RING BOOKS

You'll need:

- cardboard cut to page size
- clip rings   •   2-hole punch

PUNCH HOLES IN PAGES

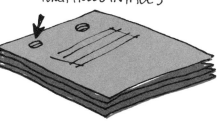

1. Mark the middle point on one side of each sheet of cardboard.
2. Punch holes with the middle of the punch on those mid-point marks.
3. Insert the rings, one in each set of holes.

And there you have it - a loose-leaf notebook.

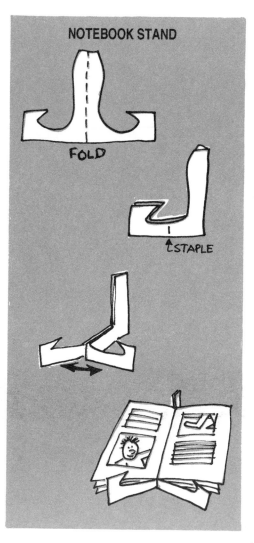

NOTEBOOK STAND

FOLD

STAPLE

FACT SHEETS

Maybe you've made a model, or a poster, or a time line, and you want people to know more about the topic.

Create a fact sheet. A fact sheet can add a lot of interest to your project.

Fact sheets can be:
- any shape you like
- any size you like
- crammed full of information
- to show key facts only

1. Once you decide what you want your fact sheet to do, choose a sheet of paper or board and cut it to the size you want.

2. Do a draft to sort out your facts and check that they fit.

3. Hand letter or type the final copy.

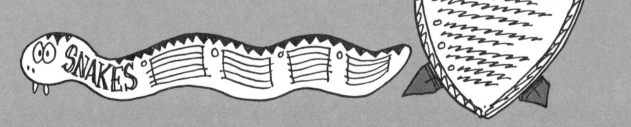

You can put your fact sheet in an old picture frame, or you can make a cardboard sheet stand up like this:

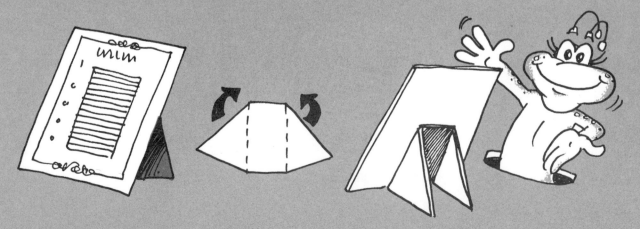

Or, you can pin your sheet on a wall near your project.

REAL LIVE VIDEO

If you want your project to really stand out, you may want to try real
video. Some families and some schools have video cameras. This
means that you can make your own color movies (with sound).
Some play back by connecting the camera to the television set.
Others play back on an ordinary videocassette recorder (VCR).

As with every project you'll ever do, you'll need a plan. Because you
may have use of the video camera for a short time, you'll need a very
good plan.

- What action do you want to catch on film?
- Plan your shots with a "story board" (see page 7).
- Decide how your video will sound.
  Will you narrate it or will you record the people in it?

- a video camera
- a videocassette to fit the camera
- a script
- a "story board"
  and, probably, an assistant.

1. Get an experienced adult to work with you on using the camera.
2. Practice getting the kind of shots you want - distance or close up.
   Practice holding the camera steady.
3. Film in "chunks" - don't try to do too much at once.
4. Remember the *pause* button is useful.
5. Follow your script and film a few mintues of each thing you want
   to show. (Moving the camera slowly is often the secret.)

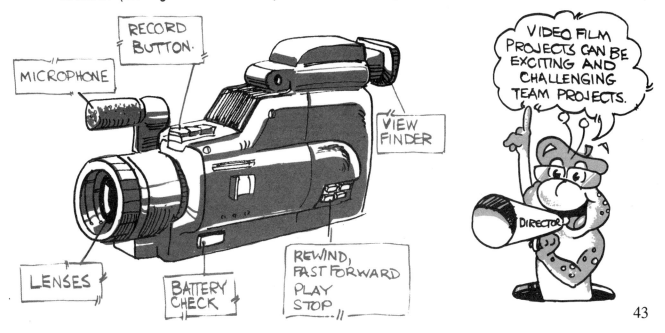

MICROPHONE

RECORD
BUTTON.

VIEW
FINDER

LENSES

BATTERY
CHECK

REWIND,
FAST FORWARD
PLAY
STOP

VIDEO FILM
PROJECTS CAN BE
EXCITING AND
CHALLENGING
TEAM PROJECTS.

DIRECTOR

WHAT'S ON TV?

Television may be the best way to get your project across. Well, not the one you watch every day, but one that YOU make.

It is great for subjects that can be illustrated. (Go back to page 7. You'll see how it works for something like "The Life Story of the Butterfly").

Television is good for telling stories, too. Suppose you decide to tell an adventure story about your family pet.

You'll need:

- a big sheet of paper for your "story board"
- a cardboard box with the flaps taped firmly shut
- 2 dowels, 4 inches (10 cm) longer than the width of the box
- a cutting knife to make a "screen"
- paints and felt pens
- long strips of paper (a bit wider than your TV "screen")
- sheets of paper - just the size of your "screen"
- maybe, a cassette recorder

1. First write a draft of the story (your first "go" at it).

2. Draw a "story board". (Rough out the pictures you'll see on your "screen".)
3. Decide what medium you're going to use for the finished pictures. Paints? Crayons? Felt pens?
4. Decide whether you will use a cassette recorder to tell the story; if not, you can write the text as captions on your "film".
5. Make your title sheet first - the name of your story and the writer.
6. On sheets of paper write chunks of the text in big clear lettering.
7. For each section of your story, make a picture to follow it. Keep going until the story is told.
8. Carefully glue the sheets down in order on your long strips of paper - your "film". Join the strips.

LOOKING AFTER KITTY
by Tom Katz

My cat's name is Kitty. He is very happy, healthy and handsome. He is a Siamese pure bred cat.

When Kitty was little we fed him calcium and vitamins so that he would grow up strong.

Kitty grew so quickly that it seemed no time before we had to buy him a new basket.

9. Take the box and carefully cut out one plain side.
10. On the other plain side, cut out your "screen" shape.
11. Make two round holes for the dowels on the sides, above and below the "screen", close to the front.

12. Decorate the box and put the dowels through the holes.
13. Glue the end of the "film" onto the lower dowel. Let it dry.

14. Roll the film by turning the lower dowel, until you get to the start.
    Put that edge over the top dowel and glue in place. Let it dry.
    You "roll" your film by turning both dowels at once in the same direction.

MAKING MODEL PEOPLE

When you are making displays or dioramas (see page 38), you may want to include people. The simplest way is to make cardboard cut outs.

You'll need:

- fairly stiff cardboard
- crayons, felt pens or paints
- scissors and strong glue

1. Trace or draw the shape of the person. Color the clothing and other features.
2. For the stand, cut a piece of cardboard the same length as the person and about the same width.
3. Crease and fold the cardboard as shown in the diagram. Cut as indicated.
4. Squeeze the stand together and glue firmly onto the back of your model. The "feet" should stick out level with the feet of the model.

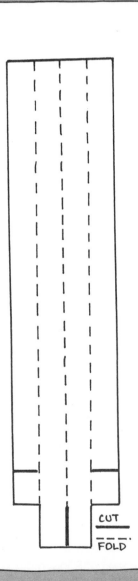

CUT
FOLD

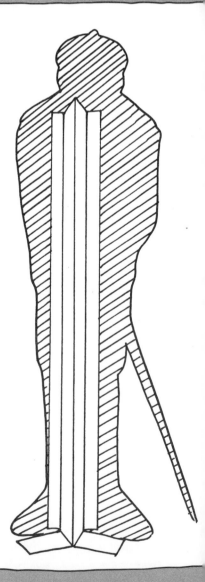

DRESSING THEM UP

Suppose your project is about fashion through the ages. You could research what people wore in, say, 1860 and decide to make a cutout model on which you can put pieces of clothing.

You'll need:

- stiff cardboard to make your models and stands
- strong paper for the "clothing"
- pencils, crayons or paints
- scissors and strong glue

1. Trace and cut out two body shapes, and use one for the female (F) and one for the male (M).

2. Trace or draw each piece of clothing, making sure it will fit your models. Leave tabs for holding the garments in place. Color and cut out each piece.

3. Make stands for your figures (see page 46) and layer the clothing on by folding the tabs over the edges of the models.

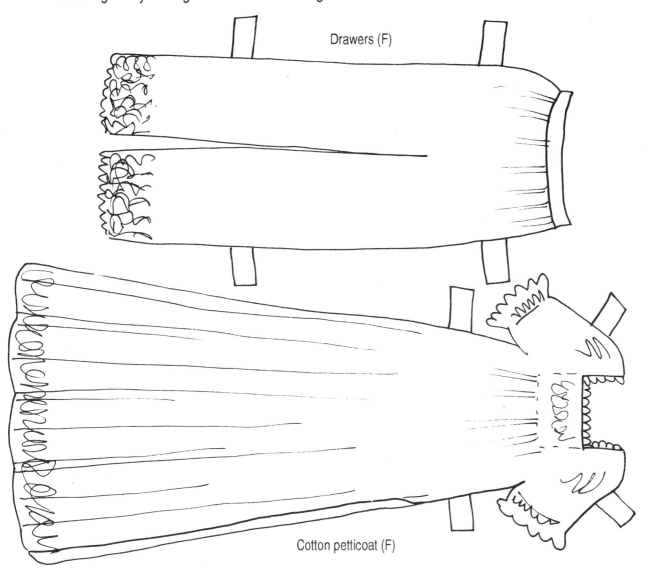

Drawers (F)

Cotton petticoat (F)

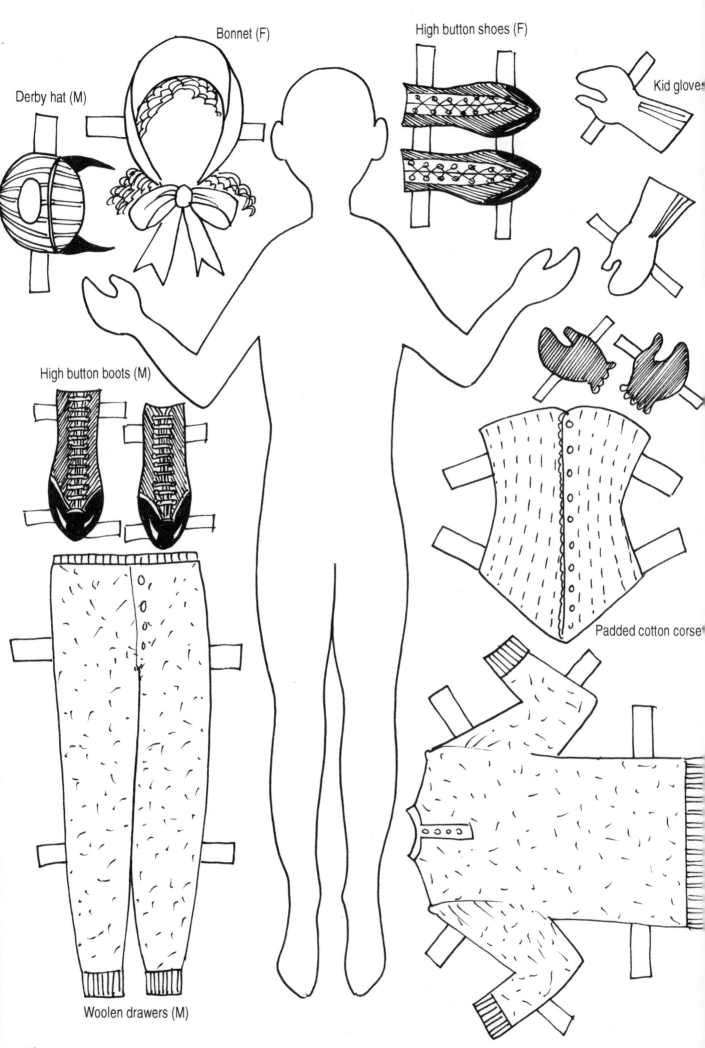

Derby hat (M)

Bonnet (F)

High button shoes (F)

Kid gloves

High button boots (M)

Padded cotton corset

Woolen drawers (M)

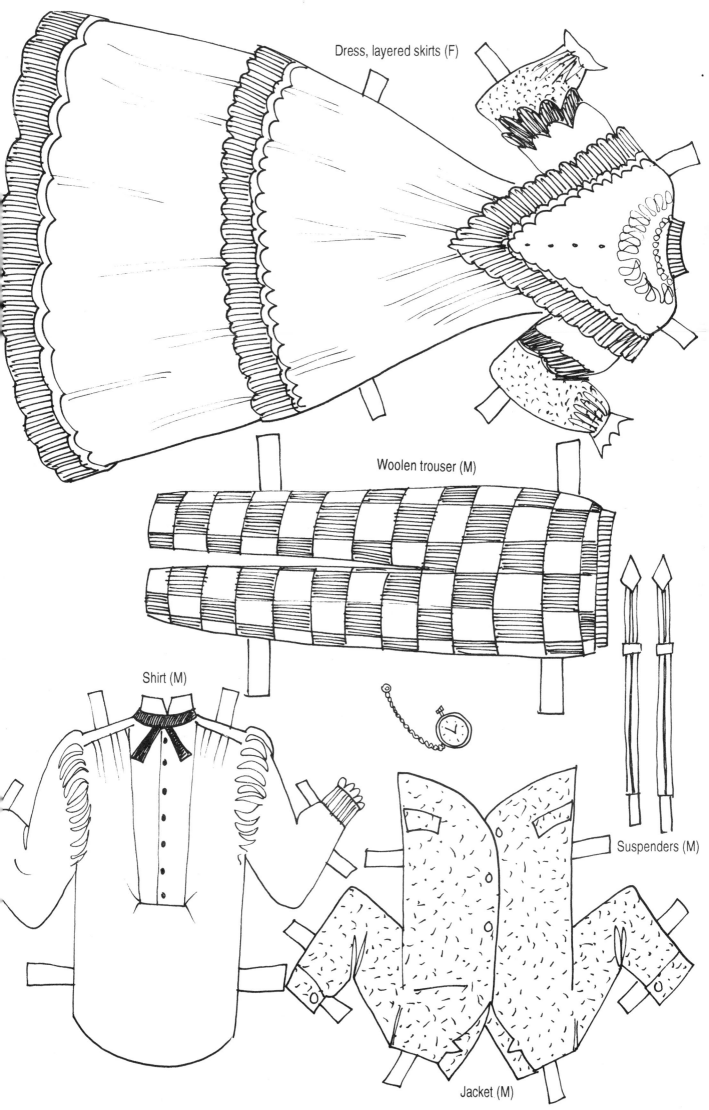

Dress, layered skirts (F)

Woolen trouser (M)

Shirt (M)

Suspenders (M)

Jacket (M)

GETTING ALL WIRED UP

Wire is great for forming the basic shapes of anything you want to model. Wire lets you make 3-dimensional models. It lets you show movement in them.

First let's try making a person.
You'll need:

- pliable wire (check out your workshop or garage, or ask at your local hardware store)
- wire cutters

1. Bend and twist lengths of wire until you get the head, body and feet right. Add arms and legs. You can make body parts separately and join them with wire twists. (Check out a real person to see how long the legs and arms are compared with the body. This is the secret of getting the shapes right.)
2. Try different action poses.

Reach

Dancing

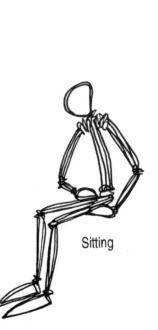
Sitting

Running

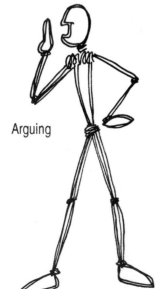
Arguing

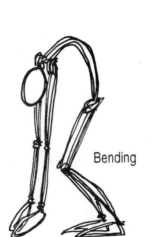
Bending

Skiing

50

3-D, THE PAPIER–MÂCHÉ WAY

Torn paper, soaked in paste or glue, can be built layer on layer to give your wire frames shape. You press layers one on the other. When the glue dries, the paper surface goes hard. You can then paint and dress your model. This is called papier–mâché.

You've made a wire frame of a person. Now let's give it "body".

You'll need:

- wire frame in the shape of a person. (Try to spread the wire to give the model shape and make the feet firm enough for it to stand on.)
- a pot of paste or glue (wallpaper paste is best)
- a hair dryer can help in drying between layers
- lots of paper strips and pieces
- fine sandpaper
- wool for hair

1. Soak the paper in paste until they soften a bit.
2. Take strips and wind them around the body, head, arms and legs to "fatten up" your model. Press the gluey paper firmly.
   Repeat until model is covered with a layer of paper.
3. Allow to dry. (This is where a hair dryer can come in handy.)
4. Add another thick layer of gluey paper and allow to dry. Now add another layer, padding out the parts that need it.
5. When it is completely dry (this may take many hours), gently rub off any bumps or corners with fine sandpaper.

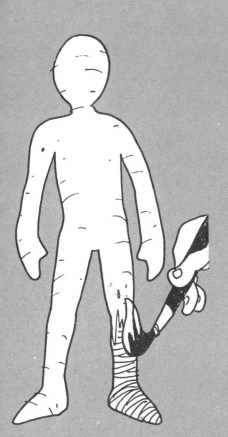

6. Paint your model a flesh color and allow to dry.

A CONICAL QUEEN
AND OTHER MODEL IDEAS

You can make models in many different ways. Sometimes your project calls for large models. Here are some ideas.

You have done your research and you want to make a model of a queen (or a king).

You'll need:

- a balloon
- baby oil or Vaseline
- papier–mâché (see page 51)
- a very large piece of cardboard
- strong glue
- paint
- wool (or curled gift ribbon) for hair
- fabric for the cloak
- silver or gold paper for the crown

1. Blow up the balloon to form the head. Tie it firmly.
2. Coat the balloon with oil or Vaseline, then layer the surface with papier–mâché and allow to dry.
3. When completely dry, let the air out of the balloon.
4. On the cardboard, draw a big circle. Cut it out and fold it in half. Cut along the fold.
5. Take half of the circle and make it into a cone. Glue or staple it.
6. Glue the balloon shape to the cone. Allow it to dry and then paint a face on it.
7. Decorate with hair, a crown and a royal cloak.

You can make models from all sorts of things. Make them as large and as interesting as you like.

TUBE MAN

EGG CARTON SHELL

CARDBOARD TOILET ROLL

CLOTH

STRONG CARD

BOX ROBOT

DRAW CIRCLES & SQUARES ON ROBOT

Hat cut from egg carton
Cardboard tube painted
Cardboard arms in slits
Painted shorts glued on
Painted legs

Collect boxes of all shapes and sizes. Glue and paint them.

PUFF

ANIMALIA

Dinosaur, dragon, alligator, kangaroo...once you get it right, you can make them all.

Animals can be made out of wire and papier–mâché, too. Use chicken wire for larger models. (But take care not to scratch yourself as you bend it.)

You'll need:

- chicken wire
- soft wire for tying bits together
- wire cutters and pliers (from the tool box)
- papier–mâché (see page 51)
- sandpaper, paint and glue

1. Squeeze the wire into the shapes you want. You can make parts such as the head separately and tie them in place with short pieces of wire.

2. Cover with papier–mâché (see page 51) and allow to dry.

3. Rub lightly with sandpaper and paint.

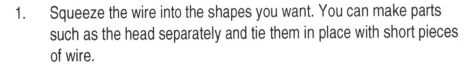

CUTOUT DORSAL BUMPS
FOLD
FROM A STRIP OF CARDBOARD

PAINT

But what about something REALLY big, such as an elephant?

1. You'll need the same things as you used for the model on page 54, with masses of papier–mâché!
2. For the elephant make a large cylinder of chicken wire.
3. Make 2 flat ears.
4. Make 4 narrow cylinders for the legs and a long one that narrows for the trunk. (Don't forget a tail!)
5. Join the parts by tying them together with bits of wire.

6. Cover with masses of papier–mâché, one layer at a time.
Allow to dry and then paint.

INSIDE OUT MODELS

When you want to show what goes on inside something, you can make "cutaway scale models". The first step is to find some reference material. A diagram of your subject is best to work from.

You'll need:

- modeling clay or play dough
- a blunt kitchen knife (and other tools for modeling)
- poster paint or broad tip felt pens

1. For each of these models, start with a diagram from a book.
2. Take a piece of clay or play dough and cut it or shape it with your hands until it is shaped like the object in your diagram.
3. Use tools to carve it or make contours and lines where you want them.
4. Color your model and add anything you like to make it look more real.
5. Make a label for your model.

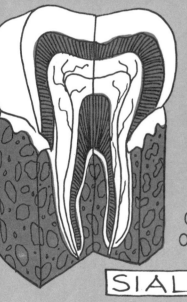

CUT AWAY
OF A TOOTH

CROSS SECTION OF A VOLCANO

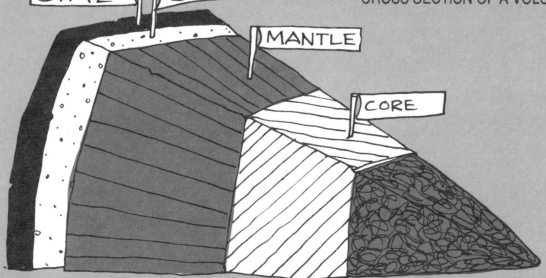

CONE SHOWING WHAT THE EARTH IS MADE OF

3-D LIVING - A MODEL PLACE

You may want your project to show what a place really looks like,
whether it's your place or a village in ancient China. There are many ways
of making models. You can use a sand tray, clay or plasticine, polystyrene
(plastic foam) or other materials.

Your "construction kit" -
Boxes of all shapes and sizes, bits of plastic, sponge, sticks, wire,
shells, small stones, silver paper, cellophane, colored cardboard,
paper, fabrics, wool, buttons,

...in fact, gather up all the crafty things you can lay your hands on

Say you live in the country and you want to make a model of your house. First,
research. Go out and study all the things you'll put in your model - the land shape,
the buildings, the trees and surrounding countryside.

House:

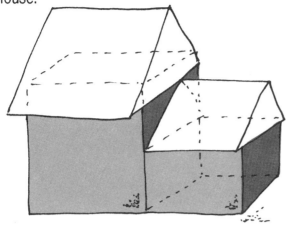

2 different -sized boxes joined for the house
Cut a box in half for the "roof"

Add details (TV aerial, chimney, etc.)
Paint and decorate

Make a tree - or three!

Wire frame

Cover with papier–mâché
(or plastic electrical tape
and then paper strips)

Paint "trunk"
Stick on bits of foam plastic
painted green for leaves
Secure to "ground" with tape

Fish pond

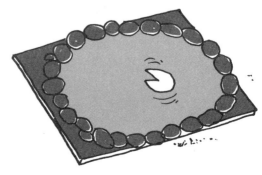

Small stones stuck around mirror or silver paper

59

To make the base of the model take a big sheet of cardboard (a flattened out box would be fine). Use chicken wire or polystyrene for the land shapes.

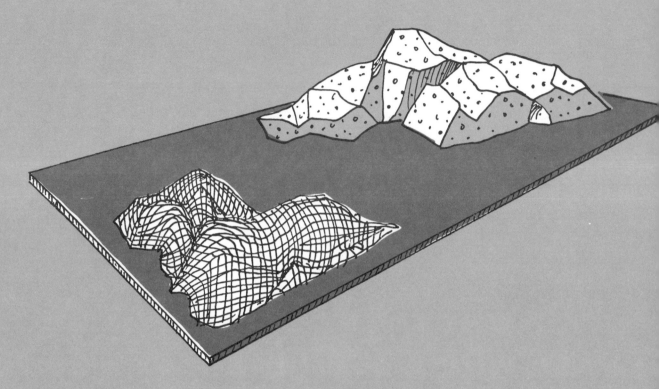

Tear up lots and lots of newspaper to make papier–mâché (see page 51). Use plenty of paste (wallpaper paste is good). Build up layers of paper and then leave them to dry.

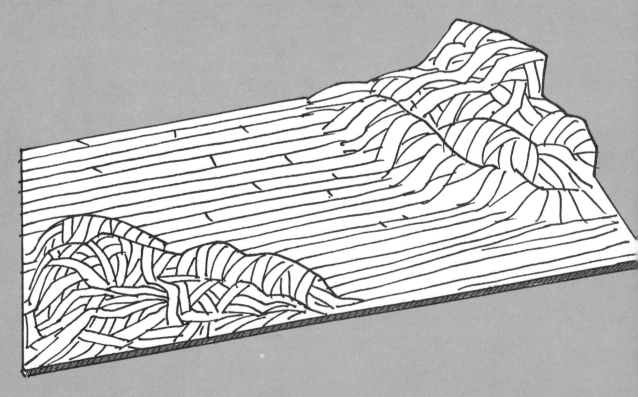

Now you can start to add things.

Carport

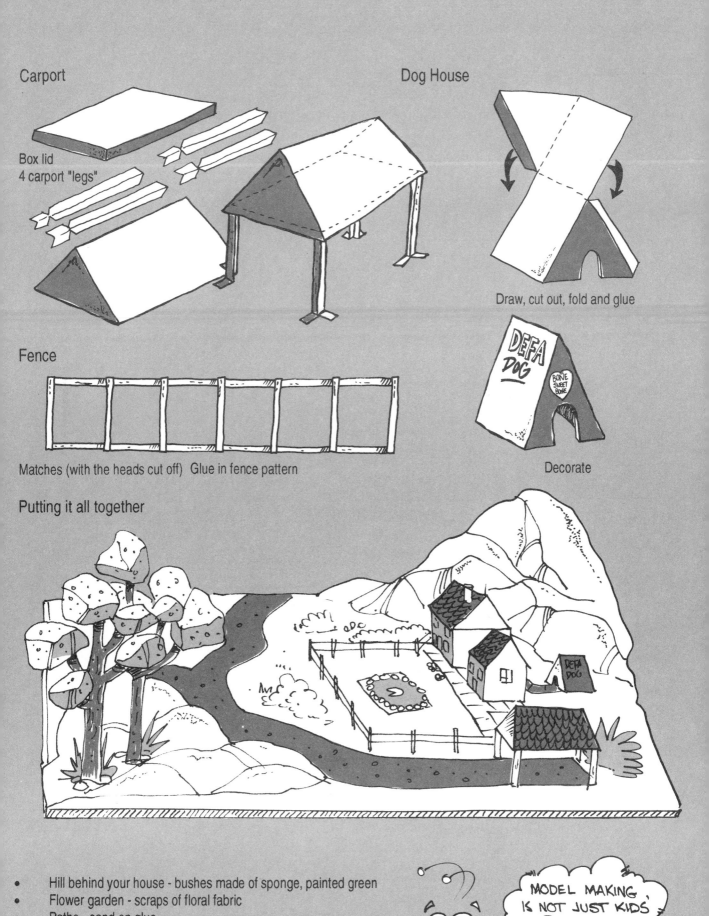

Box lid
4 carport "legs"

Dog House

Draw, cut out, fold and glue

DEFA DOG

BONE SWEET BONE

Decorate

Fence

Matches (with the heads cut off)   Glue in fence pattern

Putting it all together

- Hill behind your house - bushes made of sponge, painted green
- Flower garden - scraps of floral fabric
- Paths - sand on glue
- Long grass - old bits of rug , painted green
- Driveway - eggshells crushed and painted gray
- Small hills - crushed tissue paper: pasted, dried and painted green

MODEL MAKING IS NOT JUST KIDS' PLAY. ARCHITECTS AND TOWN PLANNERS DO IT ALL THE TIME!

PUPPET MAGIC

When it comes to capturing people's attention, you can't go past a good puppet show! You'd need to construct a simple "theater" and then write plays for your characters.

Here's one way of doing this. Check in the library for different approaches.

First make the puppets

Decide how many characters will be in your play.
You'll then need:

- cardboard tubes that fit over your finger
- tissue paper (several large sheets)
- paste for papier–mâché
- paints and things to decorate faces and make "clothes"
- tape

Tube twice as long as your finger.

Squash tissue to make "head" shape and cover with tape.

Cover ball with strips of paper covered with glue. Allow to dry.

Make "skin" as smooth as possible. Allow to dry.

Build features (nose, etc.) with bits of paper glued on.

Dress each pupp[et] differently.

Paint on features and add "hair", "earrings", etc.

Cut out costume so that it will fit your hand. Sew and put a draw string around the neck.